LAMBETH PALACE

LAMBETH PALACE

A SHORT HISTORY

GORDON HUELIN
BD, MTh, PhD, FSA

CHURCH INFORMATION OFFICE
Dean's Yard, London, SW1

First published 1974
by Church Information Office
Church House, Dean's Yard, London SW1P 3NZ
© *Central Board of Finance of the Church of England 1974*

ISBN 0 7151 4549 5

ACKNOWLEDGEMENTS

The author wishes to thank all at Lambeth Palace for
their invaluable help in the preparation of this booklet.
Thanks are also due to Messrs Seeley and Paget, Architects,
and Mrs Elizabeth Eames, FSA, of the British Museum Department of Medieval Antiquities.
Photographs by Imitor Ltd., and John R. Freeman & Co. Ltd.

Printed in England
by W & J Mackay Limited, Chatham

A FIRST GLIMPSE OF LAMBETH

Lambeth Palace, or as it was originally called the Manor of Lambeth or Lambeth House, has been the London residence of the Archbishop of Canterbury for nearly eight hundred years. In earlier days archbishops lived close to their Cathedral, but because of the growing power of the monks of the Priory of Christ Church Canterbury and the frequent disputes with them, Baldwin who was archbishop in the latter part of the twelfth century decided to move to a place where he would be free from such interference. With this in mind he exchanged some land he owned for the Manor of Lambeth then belonging to the Bishop and Church of Rochester. Baldwin himself never lived there, but his successor Hubert Walter began to build a chapel at Lambeth: a place he favoured as being within easy access of Westminster and the royal court. The Canterbury monks regarded this as a threat to their influence and appealed to the Pope, who in 1199 ordered that the building should be razed to the ground: an order which seems to have been obeyed since no trace of the twelfth century work now remains.

It was Stephen Langton, one of the greatest of the medieval archbishops who, early in the thirteenth century repaired the manor house and was probably the first to live there. From then on Lambeth House grew steadily in size though from time to time it suffered setbacks. One of these occurred in 1381 when, during the Peasants Revolt, a lawless mob stoned the gates, broke into the house and caused considerable damage. A little over a century later, Cardinal Morton built the familiar red-brick tower and gateway. Every visitor still has to pass through this gateway, and it is the part of the Palace therefore which he first sees. As a reminder of its builder's name a rain-water head on the inner-side still bears engraved upon it a 'tun'. Morton's tower is as impressive inside as out. Although the upper storeys, including what was once the Auditor's Chamber, have now been given over to the storage of archives and registers belonging to the Library, they still have fine ceilings, while the first floor room makes an impressive office—a use which it may well have had during the sixteenth century in the time of Archbishop Matthew Parker, since the name of his secretary "Alexander Nevyl" and the date 1575, May 17, are carved on one of the door jambs. The porter's lodge beside the entrance provides a reminder of a grimmer use to which this tower was formerly put: for behind it a door leads to a small room containing three heavy iron rings with an inscription or two on the wall, and this was once occupied by prisoners. From the top of Morton's tower there is a good view of the Palace buildings as a whole, as well as of the tower of what was until recently the parish church, and of the river Thames which flows past below. The name 'Lambeth' is thought to mean 'mud-haven' and serves as a reminder of the days long before the bridge was built when there was a small quay or landing-stage beside the Palace where the archbishop's barge was moored. The illustration on the title page, a reproduction of a painting to be seen in the Palace, shows how the landing-stage and Lambeth generally looked during the seventeenth century. The changes that have taken place in the life and appearance of the Palace between then and now will become apparent in the pages which follow.

Lollards' Tower and the Great Hall from the gateway

THE GREAT HALL

With the exception of the Chapel the Great Hall is the most important part of Lambeth Palace. The visitor has an impressive glimpse of its exterior on entering Morton's gateway from where it is seen to occupy almost the entire length of the outer court (*page* 4). From the main courtyard of the Palace there is a view of the east side with a fig tree in front of it reputed to be grown from shoots planted by Cardinal Pole in the sixteenth century (*page* 6). The building of the first Great Hall is believed to have been begun about the year 1200. It was completed during the time of Archbishop Boniface (1245–70), and improved and repaired by Archbishop Chichele in the fifteenth century. From the fourteenth until the mid-nineteenth century it was the scene of sumptuous banquets. Archbishop Winchelsey (1294–1313), though extravagent in his hospitality, distributed what was left over from the banquets amongst the poor who crowded round the Palace gate. This provision became known as the 'Lambeth Dole' and continued to be given until last century. There also took place in the Great Hall those Consecration feasts, the most lavish of which was the one given in honour of William of Wykeham when he was made Bishop of Winchester in 1367. The Great Hall was the meeting place of several Councils of the English Church as well as on two occasions of Convocation. During the sixteenth century Erasmus and Holbein were welcomed there by Archbishop Warham. Cranmer was particularly generous with his hospitality and entertained numerous guests in the Great Hall where there were three tables plentifully furnished. Here too, in the reign of Henry VIII under Cranmer's presidency, was held the special Commission appointed to extort from the London clergy the oath acknowledging the King's Supremacy of the Church instead of that of the Pope. The present Great Hall is often called "Juxon's Hall" from the fact that it was William Juxon who as first archbishop after the Restoration rebuilt it at his own expense after it had been left "a heap of ruins" by the regicide Colonel Scot, who during the Interregnum demolished it and sold the materials by auction. In spite of the advice of his friends, Juxon rebuilt the Hall in the medieval style and provided money for its completion should he die first. Samuel Pepys in his Diary records how, on 22 July 1665 he walked to Lambeth and "viewed the new hall, a new old-fashioned hall as much as possible: begun and means left for the ending of it by Bishop Juxon".

From the centre of its roof rises an elegant lantern carrying a vane on which are the arms of Archbishop Juxon surmounted by a mitre. On the wall on the west side a rain-water head also bears Juxon's arms and the date 1663. In order to appreciate Juxon's nobly-proportioned building one must go inside the Hall. Its most striking feature is a magnificent oak hammer-beam roof (*page* 7). Who was actually responsible for the rebuilding of this new old-fashioned hall and roof is unknown. The name of Sir Christopher Wren has been suggested since many of the details are reminiscent of his hand. Although during the Second World War more than half of the roof was destroyed, it had been completely restored by 1948 with as much as possible of the original wood being used in the reconstruction work. Other reminders of Archbishop Juxon in the Hall are the original doorway with the inscription "Anno Domini MDCLXIII", above which are his arms, and the seventeenth century carving of a negro's head (*page* 8) on either side of the overmantle at the north end, copied from those arms. There is also in a glass frame a pair of gloves which according to tradition were given to the bishop by King Charles I on the scaffold in Whitehall (*page* 8).

In spite of Juxon's splendid restoration the Great Hall was put to little use until the early nineteenth century. In the report which he made for Archbishop Howley in 1829, the architect Edward Blore described it as "a noble room, sound in all its parts, but very dirty and neglected and applied to no useful purpose". At Blore's suggestion Howley converted it into the Library with projecting bookcases or 'wings' and alcoves running down on both sides. Incendiary bombs and water wrought havoc in 1941 and many books were either lost or else seriously damaged. In the postwar re-planning the bookcases, as the photograph shows, were placed against the walls. By this means the Great Hall was restored more closely to its appearance in Juxon's day. It is now used not only as a library but also on occasions for such important events as the assembly of bishops from all over the world for what is known as the Lambeth Conference which meets every ten years. Today the Great Hall of Lambeth Palace presents a setting worthy of its historic past and at the same time serves a most useful purpose for present needs.

Great Hall

Great Hall (*interior*)

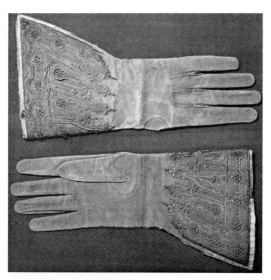

THE LIBRARY

Lambeth Palace Library, a considerable section of which is housed in the Great Hall, has a history going back several centuries. In the later Middle Ages Archbishop Chichele had a room he called a library. Later on the scholarly Cranmer possessed a collection of books which included some rarities, and he encouraged others with similar interests to make use of them. The actual foundation of the Library as such, and the opening of it to a wider public dates from 1610 when Archbishop Bancroft bequeathed "all my books in my study over the cloisters unto my successors and to the archbishops of Canterbury successively for ever". Bancroft's books included not only his own but also those belonging to some of his distinguished predecessors. Archbishop Abbot who succeeded him added many more volumes though some of these were borrowed by King James I and never returned! The example set by these two seventeenth century archbishops as benefactors to the Library was followed by their successors, some of whom made generous gifts of manuscripts and pamphlets. When Peter the Great visited Lambeth early in the eighteenth century he was so impressed by its Library that he was led to remark that he had "never imagined there were so many printed volumes in the world". Lambeth possesses the finest collection of records relating to the Church of England in existence. Among the most important of its thousands of archives are the registers of the Archbishops of Canterbury forming an almost complete sequence from the time of Pecham (1279) to the present day. There are also many volumes of their private papers and correspondence. Other volumes of papers like the Fulham Papers which consist of correspondence to the Bishop of London reflect the influence exerted by the Anglican Church in the American Colonies during the late seventeenth and eighteenth centuries. The printed books, including pamphlets, number around 150,000. In addition there is a rich collection of manuscripts amounting to nearly 3000 in all, and the earliest of which are the MacDurnan Gospels written in Ireland in the ninth century. Today Lambeth Palace Library is one of the principal national libraries in England. Its reading-room provides excellent facilities for research and is used by accredited students from this country and from many other parts of the world.

Seventeenth century carving of a negro's head

Gloves traditionally given by Charles I to Bishop Juxon

SOME LIBRARY TREASURES

Of the many treasures in the Library one of the most valuable is the famous Lambeth Bible written and illuminated about 1150. It is a superb example of English Romanesque art. The page shown (*right*) is to be found at the beginning of the Old Testament book of the prophet Isaiah. It depicts the Tree of Jesse and illustrates one of the better known prophecies of the coming of Christ. Jesse lies at the foot of the tree, Mary stands in the centre, and Christ surrounded by seven doves symbolising the gifts of the Spirit is at the top. In the roundels are figures representing prophets, virtues, the Church and the Synagogue. The original illumination is in rich colours of gold, blue, pink and green.

Some of the volumes in the Library have magnificent contemporary bindings. One of these is a psalter (*below*) put into English metre by Archbishop Matthew Parker. Another beautifully bound volume is entitled *Christian Prayers and Meditations*, which was published in 1569 and once belonged to Queen Elizabeth I. A picture in the front of it shows the queen at her private devotions (*below right*).

Lambeth Bible

Matthew Parker psalter

Prayer Book belonging to Elizabeth I

Detail of guard room roof

THE GUARD ROOM

The Guard Room of Lambeth Palace (*opposite*) by its name conjures up memories of medieval days when the archbishop of Canterbury lived like a feudal lord and kept retainers to defend himself and his property. How necessary this was is clear from the attack of the mob on Archbishop Sudbury in 1381. By the fifteenth century conditions had changed, and the Guard Room was transformed into an armoury decorated with coats of mail and weapons of every kind. Remnants of these were to be seen until the time of Archbishop Herring (1747–57). In the eighteenth century the Guard Room became the dining-room. One important event believed to have taken place in the Guard Room was the examination of Sir Thomas More by the Lords of the Council following his refusal to take the oath of Supremacy in 1534. Another was the meeting there of the first Lambeth Conference under the presidency of Archbishop Longley in 1867.

Although the Guard Room underwent extensive restoration in 1829, the arch-braced roof of wagon type was preserved intact. It was propped up until the new walls were in position to receive it. This fine roof (*above*) dating from the middle of the fourteenth century is outstanding. The other remarkable feature of the Guard Room is the collection of portraits of former archbishops which hang on its walls. They are of interest not only because of the importance of the figures they portray, but also since each one reflects the ecclesiastical fashion of his time by his appearance and the robes he wears. Thus it will be observed that the 'Canterbury' caps of the seventeenth century give place a century later to wigs. Many of the paintings are also of a high quality, being the work of such distinguished artists as Kneller, Reynolds and Romney. One which deserves particular mention is that of Archbishop Laud by Van Dyck (*page* 12). In October 1640, Laud recorded in his diary that on entering his study he found this picture lying on the floor on its face, the string by which it hung being broken, "God grant this be no omen!" he wrote. A few weeks later he was taken from Lambeth to the Tower, where he remained a prisoner until his execution.

Guard room

Corbel in the Guard Room

Archbishop Laud by Van Dyck

Some of the corbels which support the roof of the Guard Room are amusing like the one shown here (*above left*) of a woman who is possibly suffering from the agonies of toothache and clutches her jaw with both hands. A number of solid oak dining tables adorn the room, of which the largest and finest (*below*) is a splendid example of the joiner's and carver's craft in the early seventeenth century. It has a strapwork frieze and four carved lion supports to form the legs.

Seventeenth century dining table

THE RESIDENTIAL WING

Dominating the main courtyard of the Palace is a Victorian building in the perpendicular Gothic style (*below*) which forms the wing where the archbishop resides and has his administrative offices. From the end of the seventeenth until the early nineteenth century, successive archbishops made alterations and additions to the domestic buildings at Lambeth until by 1829 they had become what was then described as "a patch-work jumble". In January of that year, Archbishop Howley received a long and detailed report from an architect Edward Blore. This is still preserved in a scrap-book at the Palace, and contains the architect's summing-up in these words: "I find in almost every respect Lambeth Palace to be miserably deficient; it is most desirable and proper that these deficiencies in the Palace always necessarily occupied by so distinguished a person as the Archbishop of Canterbury should be supplied". As a result, Blore, with Howley's approval proceeded to demolish about half the then existing buildings including the picturesque manor-house which he replaced by an entirely new building with a central tower in Bath stone at very considerable expense. Sir Walter Scott on his last visit to London went to inspect the repairs then taking place at Lambeth, and was greatly pleased to see work being done "in the best Gothic style", with "the splendour of church architecture returning again". Another writer of the period spoke of the "imposing battlemented frontage". In spite of these praises people now are critical of the nineteenth century alterations. They are shocked at what was the ruthless destruction of many features including the medieval cloisters, which nowadays would almost certainly have been carefully preserved and restored. Part of the interior of Blore's building was destroyed during the Second World War but the exterior remains unharmed.

What those who come to Lambeth Palace today discover is that behind that exterior and the door with imposing flight of steps leading up from it, is not merely the London residence of the Archbishop of Canterbury and his wife, but a home where thousands of visitors from both this country and abroad enjoy hospitality and a warm welcome.

Residential wing

Picture Gallery

THE CLOISTER AND PICTURE GALLERY

From medieval times the Great Cloister at Lambeth Palace occupied a site on the south side of the Chapel. As we have already seen, this was swept away during the rebuilding of the early nineteenth century. The kitchen and domestic offices which then replaced it have, since the Second World War, been redesigned to serve the needs of the Library. They give access to a pleasant courtyard with grass and seats where students may enjoy the beauty and peace of the surroundings. Until 1829 the Picture Gallery (*above*) which now surrounds two sides of the small courtyard stood above the cloister. It was in this gallery that early in the seventeenth century Archbishop Bancroft used to confer with his clergy amongst his books and manuscripts. Later in the same century the gallery was restored by Archbishop Sheldon and was adapted by him to re-house the library bequeathed by Bancroft, which he himself had managed to retrieve from Canterbury where it had been transferred for safety during the interregnum.

The one great moment in the history of the gallery occurred in the reign of Elizabeth I on a Wednesday in Lent of 1573, when the queen had invited herself to spend a day or two at Lambeth. A pulpit was placed near the pump which stood in the open quadrangle, and from this Dr. Pearce one of the archbishop's chaplains preached the customary Lent sermon. Elizabeth who was accompanied by nobles and courtiers listened to the sermon from the gallery, while the people who filled the courtyard below "divided their attention between Her Majesty and the preacher". The archbishop who entertained and lodged the queen and her attendants on this occasion at his own expense was Matthew Parker. He and his wife Margaret, who was sometimes referred to as "Her Grace", and who died in 1570, were both concerned with the domestic life of the Palace and drew up careful rules for the running of the household and the entertainment of visitors. Although Elizabeth I strongly disapproved of married clergy, Margaret Parker's graciousness and care in seeing that her royal guest was given every attention on an earlier occasion must have moved the queen: for in bidding farewell to her hostess she is reputed to have said, "Madam I may not call you; mistress I am ashamed to call you; so I know not what to call you; yet I thank you".

THE PICTURE GALLERY

A portrait of Matthew Parker which hangs in the picture gallery shows him reading a book and surrounded by various objects including a casket and an hour-glass (*right*). It perhaps reflects Parker's special antiquarian interests. It probably dates from 1572 and is the work of an artist Richard Lyne who was one of the engravers employed by that archbishop at Lambeth.

Another portrait in the gallery is that of Thomas Cranmer (*page* 16). Unlike an earlier and better known picture of him in the palace, Cranmer is shown here with the silvery beard which he allowed to grow as a sign of mourning for Henry VIII. His melancholy appearance is in keeping with the word "Martir" inscribed on the painting and is a reminder of his last unhappy days at Lambeth before his imprisonment and death under Mary Tudor. There is a fine picture of Cranmer's predecessor William Warham who was at Lambeth from 1503 until 1532, and while there became unwillingly involved in promoting the English Reformation. His portrait was painted by Hans Holbein in 1527 during a visit by the artist to this country. It is said that it was presented to the archbishop either by Holbein or by his patron Sir Thomas More. During the troubles of the Commonwealth period it was lost but was later found and given to Archbishop Sancroft. While Warham was archbishop, there took place at Lambeth the unique and impressive ceremony of the creation of two dukes and two earls by King Henry VIII.

Several centuries separate these paintings from that of William Temple (*right*), who was archbishop from 1942 until 1944. He arrived at the palace during the Second World War when most of it had already been badly damaged. The living and office accommodation was limited, and while a beautiful chapel had been designed by Mr. Cachemaille Day, it was only a temporary one. Although Temple died after being at Lambeth for just two years, he was a great archbishop. As scholar, social reformer, teacher and worker for Christian unity his contribution was immense. Above all he was a contemporary archbishop. Nothing more clearly illustrates the contrast between the way of life at Lambeth in the past and in modern days than the glimpse of John Potter in the eighteenth century riding out from the palace in a coach escorted by six footmen and William Temple hurrying to catch a bus.

Archbishop Parker

Archbishop William Temple

THE CHAPEL

Of all the buildings at Lambeth it was the Chapel which received the earliest mention, and it is the Chapel which has ever since remained the focal point and is at the heart of all the life and work of the Palace today. While it is used by the archbishop for daily services, Lambeth Palace Chapel is not a private one but belongs to the whole Anglican Communion. In style it bears resemblances to Salisbury Cathedral and to the Temple Church in London. Records show that it was repaired by Henry III in time for the arrival of Archbishop Boniface in 1245. The only survival of the thirteenth century building is the fine doorway (*opposite*), with the arms of Archbishop Laud, through which the Chapel is still entered. Lambeth Palace Chapel has mirrored many of the important events and changes in the history of the English Church over the ages. In 1378, John Wycliffe, accused of holding heretical doctrines was summoned to give an account of himself before the bishops assembled in the Chapel. The desire of many devout people to lavish gifts on the House of God, which was so much in evidence during the later Middle Ages, found expression at Lambeth in its generous benefactor, Cardinal Morton, who filled the windows with beautiful stained glass.

A room above the present vestry on the north-east side was used by Archbishop Cranmer (*below*), and there he may have compiled the first Book of Common Prayer. Within the Chapel early on a December morning in 1558 in the presence of four officiating bishops each robed differently and so testifying to the unsettled state of the Anglican Church at that time, Matthew Parker was consecrated as the first archbishop of the reign of Elizabeth I. He was to be the architect of what became known as the "Elizabethan Settlement" and on his death was buried beneath the Chapel floor. William Laud on arriving at Lambeth found the Chapel in a sorry state especially its windows which he described as "all shameful to look on, all diversely patched like a poor beggar's coat". With customary zeal he set things in order, and inserted in one of the windows a crucifix—a charge which was afterwards brought against him by his enemies. The Puritans took their revenge by smashing every pane of glass and putting the Chapel to secular uses. With the return of Charles

II, Archbishop Juxon restored the Chapel once more. Before long however, it witnessed yet another unhappy episode in the life of the English Church when the leader of the Nonjurors, Archbishop Sancroft, celebrated Holy Communion for the last time.

With the growing missionary interest and expansion of the nineteenth century, numerous bishops were consecrated in the Chapel for work overseas. Destroyed during the Second World War except for its outer walls, it was most carefully restored by the architects Lord Mottistone and Mr Paul Paget, and on 19 October, 1955 was rededicated by Archbishop Geoffrey Fisher in the presence of the Queen and other members of the Royal Family. Since then it has played its part in the ecumenical movement for, with the encouragement of Dr Michael Ramsey, many distinguished churchmen of other religious communions and denominations have shared in acts of worship within its walls.

Archbishop Cranmer

Thirteenth century doorway of the Chapel

THE RESTORED CHAPEL

The restored Chapel of Lambeth Palace (*opposite*) is now closer to its original appearance than at any other time in its history. In the seventeenth century Archbishop Laud removed the vaulted ceiling and substituted for it a flat panelled one of wood which was painted and adorned with his arms. This in turn was replaced in 1829 by Archbishop Howley with a high groined roof of wood and plaster. The architects Lord Mottistone and Mr. Paul Paget, in their reconstruction of the Chapel after its devastation during the Second World War,

Seventeenth century chapel screen

not only preserved the walls but also added the lofty vaulted roof which was probably a feature of the original structure. In order to reveal the beauty of the medieval builders further, they removed some of the embellishments made by the nineteenth century Archbishop Tait. As more seating accommodation was needed in the new Chapel, the elaborately carved screen at the west end (*above*) which had been added during Laud's time (*see pp. 10 and 12*) and had suffered little damage, was re-erected outside the west door in what is known as the Post Room (from a large wooden post now removed), where it separates the Chapel entrance from a robing-room. A careful study of the records relating to the subjects contained in Cardinal Morton's fifteenth century windows was also made. These subjects which were taken from the *Biblia Pauperum* and showed events in the life of Christ accompanied by Old Testament incidents foreshadowing them have been reproduced in modern stained glass by the artists Carl Edwards and Hugh Powell. Those depicted in the east window are the offering of Isaac, the penitent thief, Christ on the cross, the unrepentant thief and the lifting up of the brazen serpent in the wilderness.

The Chapel is furnished with gifts from almost all the churches of the Anglican Communion. A most generous donation from the American Episcopal Church provided the new organ. Richly bound and gilded prayer and hymn books can be seen in the pews. At the west end of the Chapel where since the fifteenth century the window had been obstructed by the Lollards' Tower a small music gallery was formed to hold a choir and the organ console. For this purpose an oriel window, first installed by Archbishop Juxon and decorated with his arms, was lowered. Over the door inside the Chapel are the arms of Dr Geoffrey Fisher who was Archbishop in October 1955 when it was rededicated, and who at the most solemn moment of that service spoke these words: "In the faith of Jesus Christ we dedicate again this ancient chapel, now after the ravages of war, restored and refurnished for its sacred use to the glory of God and the perfecting of the worship of His people".

Chapel

Seventeenth century bench end

Not everything to be found in the Chapel today is new. Some of the woodwork which suffered damage during the war of 1939–45 has since been repaired with such skill that it is difficult to distinguish the new work from the original. When William Laud arrived at Lambeth in 1633 he set up in front of the altar what one of his opponents described as "a new costly rail". At each end of the sanctuary sections of this may be seen, while along the walls at the east end of the Chapel are most of the carved wooden pews that were also commissioned by him. Each pew-end bears a cherub's head with other decoration (*left*). Laud replaced the medieval tiles of the Chapel floor with the black and white marble ones which are still in position. However, just above the step where, until the postwar restoration, stood his screen, a few of the original tiles can now be seen. They are four inches square and belong to a group known as the "Westminster" tiles, since examples are present in the muniment room of Westminster Abbey where they are known to have been in existence by the reign of Richard II (1377–1399). The tiles at Lambeth include the Royal Arms with three lions reversed, a stag being attacked by a hound, one of a four-tile patterned cross within a circle, and a delightful lion (*below*).

Medieval tile

In 1903 Randall Davidson became archbishop. Twenty-five years earlier he had been married in the Chapel to Edith Tait the daughter of one of his predecessors to whom he was then Chaplain. A silver wedding present subscribed to by their friends was used to enrich the sanctuary of the Chapel with three marble steps of white (for sincerity), black (for contrition) and porphyry or red (for love), the colour of the steps to Purgatory in Dante's vision. The altar of the restored Chapel is rather longer than the Victorian one which meant that the three steps had to be slightly altered in their position. But they are still in place.

Outside the Chapel in what was formerly the Post Room stands a brass lectern in memory of Mary Eleanor Benson, daughter of Archbishop Benson. It has the date October 1890, and the well-known words of the Burial Service in a slightly altered order: "In the midst of death we are in life".

A few treasures which are also associated with the Chapel or with religious purposes are now kept in show-cases in the Cloister Gallery. These include a set of Eucharistic vestments (*right*) which belonged either to Cardinal Pole, the last Roman Catholic archbishop of Canterbury, or to one of his chaplains. Although they are more than four hundred years old these vestments are strikingly modern in their appearance. Another display case houses a red and gold cope known as the "Davidson Cope", because it was worn by Randall Davidson as Bishop of Winchester at the Coronation of Edward VII, and later as Archbishop of Canterbury at the Coronation of George V. There is also a magnificent white cope and mitre which were provided by laymen of the Church in Japan and worked by craftsmen of that Church using Japanese fabrics, silks and brocades. In 1948 when Bishop Yashiro, Presiding Bishop of the Church in Japan came to the Lambeth Conference, he presented the cope and mitre to Dr Geoffrey Fisher the then archbishop of Canterbury, as a sign that the fellowship between his Church and the see of Canterbrry interrupted but never broken by the years of war was once again fully renewed. It was this cope and mitre which Dr Fisher wore at the Coronation of Queen Elizabeth II in Westminster Abbey on 2 June 1953.

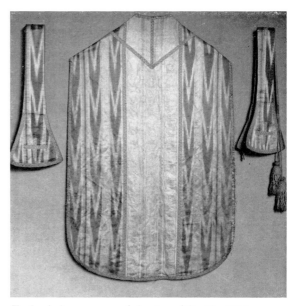

Eucharistic vestments of the time of Cardinal Pole

Also in the Gallery there is a beautiful ivory cup (*right*) said to be of German workmanship, and thought to have been used by Archbishop Laud as a chalice before his execution in 1645. Some items in the Gallery show-cases have other interests. Among them is a display of electro-types of coins minted by archbishops of Canterbury from the eighth until the sixteenth century when their right to mint ceased. The earliest bears on one side the name of archbishop Jaenberht, who died in 790, and that of his overlord Offa, king of Mercia on the other. The last was struck in the reign of Henry VIII and is inscribed TC for Thomas Cranmer or possibly Thomas Cantuariensis. Another object to be seen is a tortoise shell. This is all that remains of the tortoise placed in the Palace garden by Archbishop Laud in 1633. It survived until 1753 and might have done so even longer, had it not been, it is said, for the negligence of the gardener of the time.

German ivory cup

THE GARDEN AND
LOLLARDS' TOWER

The monks of Rochester were the first to lay out what later became the garden of Lambeth House. From then on it seems to have been well cared for. In the thirteenth century the garden was flourishing, with pears and other fruit from the orchard being on sale at the gate. Two hundred years later it boasted vines as well. Matthew Parker and his wife were specially interested in the garden and rules were set down as to the duties of the gardener, namely "to see the garden, orchard and walks to be kept well weeded and rolled, the grass walks not suffered to be much grown, but kept low with the scythe. To see that there be planted in the grounds flowers, herbs and roots, both for the provision of the kitchen and chambers; and with all sorts of good fruits, herbs, plants and flowers for use and pleasure". Subsequent archbishops made various improvements to the garden by adding trees, shrubs and greenhouses. Archbishop Tenison in the early eighteenth century built a rabbit house "without royal licence". More recently during the primacy of Archbishop Lang a donor made the unusual but valuable present of soil for the garden. Lambeth Palace garden was still in the eighteenth century on the edge of pleasant country. Nowadays, with the unending flow of traffic along the embankment and over the bridge, and with more and more buildings dominating the landscape, the garden serves as an oasis and a haven of peace.

Across the garden a view may be had of Lollards' Tower (*left*) or as it was sometimes called Chichele's Tower after its builder, or again the Water Tower since it stood beside the quay on the river. This was constructed of Kentish ragstone during the years 1434–5 when Chichele was archbishop. From this angle is seen a turret which is covered with lead and contains a bell dated 1687. On the side of the tower facing the Thames is a niche which until the reign of Henry VIII held a statue of the martyred St Thomas of Canterbury. Boatmen as they passed were accustomed to doff their caps as a mark of respect. Although incendiary bombs fell on Lollards' Tower on two separate occasions during 1940–1 causing serious damage and making the whole building uninhabitable, it has since been carefully restored.

Lollards' Tower

At the top of the stairway in Lollards' Tower is a stone doorway containing a massive door of wooden planks three inches in thickness. A further door (*right*) still has hooks and staples for padlocks, as well as a little peep-hole through which it was possible to watch those on the inner side without being observed. This door gives access to a small gloomy room (*below*). According to a long tradition this once served as a prison for the followers of John Wycliffe who were known as 'Lollards', and there were other prisoners here during the sixteenth and seventeenth centuries. The walls bear incised inscriptions consisting of names and half-finished sentences. Although badly damaged by incendiary bombs during the Second World War, there still survives part of the original wooden wainscot, with seven iron rings to which those unfortunate enough to find themselves prisoners were secured.

Doorway in Lollards' Tower

Lollards' prison

Graffiti in Lollards' prison

One of the inscriptions carved on the prison wall (*left*) in Lollards' Tower reads NOSCE TE IPSM and is curious since these words are said to have formed part of Archbishop Cranmer's motto. Below is inscribed the sacred IHS monogram, and underneath this will be found a complete set of dice.

THE CRYPT

(*Below*): The crypt may be part of the chapel built by Stephen Langton, and if so dates from the early thirteenth century. During the course of time it has been put to a variety of uses serving as a lumber room and a wine-cellar, and in two world wars as an air-raid shelter. Today it has been restored to its original condition and to an appearance more worthy of what is the earliest surviving part of that building which has played so distinguished a role in the story of the Church in this land—Lambeth Palace.

Crypt

The Reverend Doctor Gordon Huelin has for the past eleven years been Vicar of St Margaret Pattens, a Guild Church in the City which serves as a centre for Christian study. He also lectures in the Theological Department of King's College London, and for the Extra-Mural Department of London University of which he is a Member of the Senate. A Fellow of the Society of Antiquaries, he has since boyhood days been interested in London history and is a recognised authority in this field. Dr Huelin is the author of a number of books and articles on theological and historical subjects. One of these entitled *The Cross in English Life and Devotion* was commissioned by Dr Michael Ramsey as the Archbishop of Canterbury's Lent Book for 1972.

ISBN 0 7151 4549 5   price 50p